The World's Most
Beautiful Birds

By Annie Buckley

The
**Child's
World**®
www.childsworld.com

Published in the United States of America by The Child's World®
1980 Lookout Drive • Mankato, MN 56003-1705
800-599-READ • www.childsworld.com

ACKNOWLEDGMENTS

The Child's World® : Mary Berendes, Publishing Director

Produced by Shoreline Publishing Group LLC
President / Editorial Director: James Buckley, Jr.
Designer: Tom Carling, carlingdesign.com
Cover Design: Slimfilms

Photo Credits
Cover–dreamstime.com
Interior–dreamstime.com: 9, 14, 17, 21, 22, 24, 25, 28; iStock: 6, 10, 11, 13, 15, 18, 19, 27; Photos.com: 4, 15, 20, 26.

LIBRARY OF CONGRESS CATALOG-IN-PUBLICATION DATA

Buckley, Annie.
  The World's most beautiful birds / by Annie Buckley.
     p. cm. — (Reading rocks!)
  Includes index.
  ISBN-13: 978-1-59296-864-0 (library bound : alk. paper)
  ISBN-10: 1-59296-864-3 (library bound : alk. paper)
 1. Birds—Juvenile literature. I. Title. II. Series.

QL676.2B825 2007
598—dc22

                                    2007004190

CONTENTS

BOLD AND
Beautiful

Just like people, birds come in many shapes and sizes. But unlike humans, birds can be as brightly colored as a rainbow. Lime green and deep purple, brilliant yellow and fire-engine red, sunny orange and deep-sea blue—some birds' feathers look like they've been dipped in paint! Parrots and toucans **boast** many beautiful colors. Flamingos' feathers are a lovely pink. Cardinals are bright red and jays' feathers are royal blue. Peacocks' feathers are silvery green and purple.

There are nearly 10,000 different types of birds in the world. Here's a look at some of our most amazing feathered friends.

Toucans are known for their large beaks. The beaks are hollow, so they don't weigh the birds down.

Parrots and toucans have many things in common besides their bright colors. Both birds live in the rain forests of South America, Central America, and Africa. And they both have big beaks—especially toucans. Some toucans' beaks are half as big as their bodies!

The toco toucan is the most common toucan. Tocos are black and white with red and orange beaks.

Parrots' beaks aren't as big as toucans', but their voices are bigger. The word *parrot* also means to **imitate**. It comes from the way that parrots mimic, or copy, voices. African grey parrots are especially good mimics. One African grey is famous for learning 600 words!

That's One Big Parrot

The Kakapo is the heaviest parrot. It can't fly, but its song can carry farther than any other bird. The Kakapo stamps down the ground to make a hole. From inside this space, the Kakapo takes a huge breath. When it opens its mouth to sing, the song can be heard up to four miles (6 km) away!

When a peacock spreads its tail, its green, purple, blue, and gold feathers **shimmer**. The pattern of the feathers looks like dozens of eyes.

Like many kinds of birds, male peacocks have the most brilliant colors. Peacocks are a type of pheasant. Originally, they come from Asia. But peacocks have been kept as pets or in zoos all over the world, including the U.S. The most common peacock you might see is the

India blue peacock. It has a bright blue body and a patch of feathers on its head. It also has brilliant tail feathers. Green peacocks are less common.

When a peacock spreads its feathers, all "eyes" are on him!

*A hummingbird's long, thin beak is perfect for reaching a flower's tasty **nectar**.*

Hummingbirds have beautiful colors that change depending on the light. The feathers of many hummingbirds are red, green, or blue. Tiny ridges in the feathers reflect light. This makes the birds appear to be many colors at once. Because of their special wing structure, some hummingbirds look shiny, or **iridescent**.

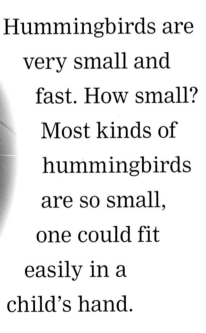

Hummingbirds are very small and fast. How small? Most kinds of hummingbirds are so small, one could fit easily in a child's hand.

How fast? Its wings beat between 40 and 60 times per second. That would be about the same as a person taking 50 steps each second! The smallest bird in the world is the bee hummingbird. Even though it's small, it's one of the fastest birds in the world.

It's a battle to see who is more colorful and beautiful: this bright hummingbird or this bird-of-paradise plant.

2

PRETTY Songs

Not only do birds have colorful feathers, they also are able to sing more beautiful and different songs than any other animal. Birds sing to communicate with one another. They use different songs to attract mates, defend their homes, or to warn about danger.

The best time to hear birds' songs is at dawn. From South American rain forests to African **savannahs**, from fields to farms, birds use this quiet time of day to sing their songs.

To sing, birds have a special **voicebox**. A bird's voicebox is located lower in the body than a person's. Birds have muscles that let their voicebox vibrate in different ways when air passes over it. This is how birds make sounds.

A special voicebox helps birds make beautiful music.

The yellow warbler is part of a large family of songbirds.

A songbird is a bird that has a very musical call. Many kinds of songbirds can be seen and heard throughout North America. Their bright colors and varied songs are common in parks, yards, woods, fields, and even playgrounds everywhere.

Eastern bluebirds have bright blue

can be seen
in fields and
grasslands in the
Eastern United
States. There are
many yellow and
red songbirds, too.
Several types of
warblers have yellow
feathers. Scarlet tanagers
have bright red
body feathers
and black wings.
Robins, of course,
have red chests.

*There are several types
of bluebirds found in
the United States.*

Whether they sing softly or screech loudly, all birds come from eggs. Birds' eggs break easily. Other animals like to eat them, too. To protect their eggs, most birds build sturdy nests. Before making a nest, males sing or dance to **attract** a female. Then they claim an area and build their nest.

This adult bald eagle guards his large nest.

The most common shape of nest for a North American songbird is a bowl. It's made of twigs and leaves, and is lined with soft grass. Other birds use different shapes and materials. Some swallows build nests in high places out of clumps of mud. They line the insides with grass or feathers. Eagles are bigger birds, so they need stronger nests. They use large sticks and branches for their nests. Eagles start by placing sticks to form triangles. Then they add more and more sticks that form more triangles. Soon, the nest is sturdy and ready to hold and protect a future soaring eagle!

Smaller songbirds usually form sticks into bowl-shaped nests to protect their eggs.

This adult swallow is feeding its babies as they wait inside a nesting box.

You can help these wild birds learn to nest in your backyard or neighborhood. To encourage birds in your neighborhood to build nests nearby, leave small pieces of string or yarn in your yard. Strings should be short, no longer than four inches (10 cm). Leave them on tree branches or across clotheslines where the birds can find them. A nesting box will also give birds a safe place to nest. Different types of birds need different kinds of nesting areas, so read up on the types of birds in your area. Then you can give them the right homes.

These babies from another swallow family are waiting for food in a homemade birdhouse.

The brightly colored yellow oriole sips nectar for a sweet treat.

Songbirds live in many places, from wide prairies to thick forests, from darkened barns to bright yards. Some songbirds live in cities, too.

Orioles travel through Central Park in New York City in spring. Mute swans raise their chicks around the park's lake. Mockingbirds often live in city gardens and parks, too.

Cities can be dangerous for birds, however. We can help keep them safe by leaving nests alone. We should also be quiet around birds so we don't scare them away.

Swans can often be seen gliding on quiet ponds in parks.

3

POWERFUL
Splendor

Some birds are beautiful because of their flying, not their feathers.

Birds of prey (also called raptors) get their name because they hunt other animals for food. Eagles, owls, and hawks are all birds of prey.

There are about 500 different kinds

of raptors. Tiny elf owls are only 5 inches (13 cm) high. Ospreys, who live near water to hunt for fish, have wings that stretch up to 6 feet (2m) across. Even bigger than that, huge Andean condors have wings that spread over 10 feet (3 m)!

Hawks are among the most common raptors. They use their wings to swoop down and snatch animals in their claws.

Since raptors are hunters, they need to be able to chase after their food. A raptor's wings must help the bird dive, float, swoop, and change directions quickly.

This red-tailed hawk stands about 2 feet (.6 m) tall but weighs only about three pounds (1.4 kg).

Forest raptors have shorter wings for steering through branches. Field raptors have broad wings that help them float while they search for food.

Once a raptor spots its victim, it swoops down and catches it with its powerful feet. Super-sharp claws called **talons** grip the meal so it doesn't get away. Then it's dinner time. The raptor flies to a safe spot. It uses its sharp, hooked beak to tear into its meaty meal. It eats the meal itself or brings pieces of the meat to its young. Soon, the babies will have to learn to hunt for themselves.

This hawk's sharp talons are perfect for grabbing prey.

In order to find their meals from high in the sky, most birds of prey have excellent vision. Owls are active at night and can see in the darkness. A special part of an owl's face is able to **detect** sounds. This way, the owl can hear an animal, even if it can't see it clearly.

"Hooo" is it? An owl can't move its eyes from side to side like you can. It must turn its whole head to see in different directions.

Have you heard the saying "eagle-eyed"? This is used to describe someone who can see very well and notices everything. It comes from the eagle's excellent eyesight. Eagles can spot fish underwater from high above the water. From the treetops, they can see a tiny rabbit hopping across a field.

Time for lunch! This eagle has just snatched a fish from the water in its sharp talons.

Spreading its enormous wings, a California condor soars above its canyon home.

No matter how beautiful a bird is, it can be threatened by human-made problems. Some birds are **endangered** and need extra protection. The California condor, for example, is "critically endangered." That means there are fewer than 50 adult birds left in the world. The land that these birds live in is getting too crowded with people for them to survive.

People who work to save birds are called **conservationists**. They try to protect birds by keeping safe places for them to live.

If you see a bird in the wild, try not to touch it. It is a lot of fun to watch beautiful birds, and you can help to keep them safe by not touching these fragile creatures.

"Conserve" means to keep for use later on. Many people are working hard to conserve nature and many animals.

Build Your Own Birdbox

Get an empty paper milk carton. Cut it in half, wash it well, and let it dry. Close the dry, clean carton with masking tape. Cover the outside of the carton with brown tape. Cut a round hole big enough for the type of bird you want to visit the box. Make smaller holes in the top and bottom of the box to let out water and steam. This keeps the box dry. Make a hanger for your box with a piece of string or wire. Now hang it in a tree and wait for your feathered visitors!

GLOSSARY

attract to appeal to others and draw them in

birds of prey birds that hunt and eat other animals

boast to brag

conservationists people who work to protect something, such as animals or areas of land

detect to notice or become aware of something

endangered to be in danger of dying out

imitate to copy someone or something

iridescent to have colors that shimmer and shine and seem to change colors in different types of light.

nectar a sweet liquid found inside some flowers

savannahs flat, grassy areas with low trees and bushes

shimmer to shine and softly wave or flicker

talons hooked claws

voicebox a special body part that helps animals make sounds

FIND OUT MORE

BOOKS

About Birds: A Guide for Children
   by Cathryn Sill (Peachtree Publishers, 1997)
   An introduction to birds from around the world.

Bird Calls (Play the Sounds, Pull the Tabs)
   by Frank Gallo (Innovative Kids, 2001)
   Listen to lots of bird calls and learn more about the birds that
   sing them.

Birds in Your Backyard
   by Barbara Herkert (Dawn Publications, 2001)
   A great guide to help you identify the birds in your area.

The Burgess Bird Book for Children
   by Thornton W. Burgess (Dover Publications, 2003)
   Written by a nature and bird expert, this great book will
   introduce you to all kinds of birds.

WEB SITES

Visit our Web page for lots of links about beautiful birds:
   www.childsworld.com/links

Note to Parents, Teachers, and Librarians: We routinely check our Web links to
make sure they're safe, active sites—so encourage your readers to check them out!

INDEX

Annie Buckley is a writer and artist who lives in Los Angeles. She is the author and illustrator of *The Kids' Yoga Deck* and the co-author of *Once Upon a Time: Creative Writing for Kids*. Annie has written four other "Reading Rocks!" books. Annie has always admired birds for their amazing ability to fly! She likes seeing birds brightening the city streets where she lives. For *Beautiful Birds*, she enjoyed learning more about these wonderful creatures, especially about the many songs birds sing all over the world.